The Musings of The Impatient Poet

Liz Goodfellow

India | USA | UK

The Musings of The Impatient Poet © 2024
Liz Goodfellow

All rights reserved.

No part of this publication may be
reproduced, stored in a retrieval system, or
transmitted, in any form or by any means,
electronic, mechanical, photocopying,
recording or otherwise, without the prior
written permission of the presenters.

Liz Goodfellow asserts the moral right to
be identified as author of this work.

Presentation by *BookLeaf Publishing*

Web: www.bookleafpub.com

E-mail: info@bookleafpub.com

ISBN: 9789360948962

First edition 2024

To you, dear reader, thank you for opening up this book and reading this page. Already, I'm very grateful.

Thank you for giving my words a chance and I hope you find some moments of joy, clarity and inspiration.

Love, Liz x

ACKNOWLEDGEMENT

I would like to thank BookLeaf Publishing, for creating a challenge to write a poem, a day, over 21 days! Being a competitive person, who enjoys a challenge and getting outside of my comfort zone, I was immediately inspired to take part. It got me writing, daily, and has provided an opportunity for my words to be shared with an audience.

I would also like to thank all the special people in my life (they know who they are), for constantly providing inspiration for my poetry. It is my love for them that has inspired most of my work.

A special acknowledgement goes to all my parents, who, in their different ways, have given me the confidence to do something with my passion, skill and enthusiasm, and inspired me with their own writing gifts and talents.

Thank you xx

PREFACE

Liz has been a teacher for twenty years and has always loved words. She has also run a business, connecting, promoting and nurturing women, who were self employed. Liz has supported others in their writing endeavours and she has used words to educate, inspire, promote and connect people.

Recently, Liz has felt compelled to express herself, through the written word, specifically, poetry. Being a lover of exercise and movement, she finds poetry an accessible and enjoyable way to craft smaller texts of meaning, with feeling, without having to be stationary for too long!

Liz also loves music and lyrics, and finds the opportunity to add rhythm and have the freedom to 'freestyle' in terms of written structure, very exciting.

One day she might write a novel, but for now, poetry is her love.

Writing For Pleasure

Writing for pleasure, oh that would be nice!
Picking up the pen, the paper and getting lost in
time.

No expectations, no "mummy, mummy" or "Mrs
Goodfellow, Mrs Goodfellow"
Sitting still can be hard for me; getting out of the
fast lane, going into the mode of slow.

Build in some daily journalling time; light that
candle - make that hot drink.
Time for planning, time for reflection - just time
to think!

Oh, writing for pleasure - putting pen to paper; it
makes those words count.
Gives them gravitas; gives them life - just lets
them all out.

So write, Lizzie, write - move those hands
across the page,
And don't be too critical of what you've done
and get excited at what you could create!

New Year Firework

You are the firework,
You are the force.
Go into this year and open those doors.
Be brave in your beauty,
Look forward, not back,
Take with you, those, who can pick up the slack.
Another year, another adventure; we are
privileged to be alive!
I wish you health, long term contentment and
resilience to grow and thrive!

You Are A Disco Ball

You bring the 'bling', the sparkle and the glitz,
To any space, situation where people are in,
You are the dazzle; the magic motion moon,
That illuminates and excites, and brings energy
to the room.

You are the disco ball, the statement piece,
Perfectly imperfect, shiny and fully lit.
People look upon you but get overwhelmed by
your light,
By this awesome orb, this celestial body -
A truly spectacular sight!

Your imperfections and cracks make you whole,
Each fragment reflecting different parts of your
soul.
And if people pause and gaze upon you, with
just a glance,
They will fall under your spell and simply
dance, dance, dance……

I Really Do Dance In My Kitchen

I really do dance in the kitchen
When no-one's there I dance, I let go and become free.
I let the music pulse through my body
I feel every beat and my body says, more please!

The vibrations ripple and tickle their way through, from outside in,
Re-igniting my passion for movement and life.
For those moments, I'm not a mum, a daughter, a friend or a wife.

I really do dance in my kitchen; it's why I bought this house.
The echo, the space - the quality of the sound.
An environment to come together; to have fun and get people round.

It starts with a sway, an uplifting - I feel I can almost fly!
It's my experience of total joy - my version of getting 'high'.

So, come and dance with me, in my kitchen,

I promise you'll not be judged.
Come and discover, connection to the music, and
to each other,
And experience powerful self love.

The Walk & Talk

Talking and walking, such a natural pairing,
Company and companionship, all while
movement making.

Side by side through forests we explore,
Each step we take, we let go a little more.

The weight of the to-do list, feels a little lighter
now,
We feel energised, connected and life's noise is a
little less loud.

Come and walk with us, outside into the beauty,
Come away from the screen, the chores and your
sense of duty.

We can even walk in silence, if that is what you
need,
Togetherness can be quiet - a wonderful
opportunity to just 'be'.

What is Friendship?

Is it the hugs, the handshakes or the many kisses,
Or the light-hearted 'cheers' and delicious dinner
party dishes?

Is it about the laughs and the fun interactive
games,
Or when it goes deeper with the sharing of each
other's dreams?

Or is it the deep feelings shared - the fears and
the tears,
And the making the effort through the many,
many years?

Is it the stories of parenting woes and the
tribulations at work that worry us so,
Or is it the banter and the pub quiz fun,
The feeling of connection - feeling more than
just a 'one'.

Over the years, we've experienced it all - dinner
parties, zip wiring, and the glam and glitzy balls.

We've dressed up; we've dressed down - we've
revealed our true selves.

The beauty and the ugliness - we know each
other so well.

Friends are the family that we choose, so the
saying goes,
But what makes friendship go the distance? I'm
not sure any us really know…

But I suggest and I believe, it's about evolving
together,
Riding the rollercoaster of life while supporting
each other's endeavours,

By lifting each other 'up' and making each other
feel good,
sometimes by a hug or simply, just a look.

Her Wonderful Wildness

Her energy is a magnet - her *wildness; her passion,

For creating, and evolving - always on a mission.

With so many dreams and so much to achieve,

So much already done, with internal self belief,

That no matter what others, think or say -

She knows her worth and value - the contribution she can make.

From one 'wild' woman to another, I say:

Never lose your 'wild'; never extinguish that flame.

For those who burn bright, inspire and give light,

To others wanting more, too - MORE from this
life.

She's on a journey - destination unknown,

Sometimes with others; sometimes alone.

Living life forwards, but learning from looking
back,

She is designing her own life; the one she is
destined to have.

A limitless life, full of love, wonder and beauty,

Full of remarkable memories, connection and
security.

Her family completes her, but she is far from
'done',

For life in the wilderness, will always be more
fun!

wildness 'the basic ability of anything living, to renew itself'

Baby Girl

Beautiful girl, you've lit up our world;
A new life, at the beginning, starting to
unfold....

A delicate rose, you were born with such ease;
To a partnership of two, that have become a
loving family of three.

To all who gaze upon you, you cast a magic
spell;
Captivating people's attention with those eyes,
smile and delicious smell.

Your love of life and of people, is already very
clear;
Your sense of humour articulated by the biggest
laugh - so deep and sincere.

As you turn one, the world awaits you - with
adventure, challenge and opportunities - so
much to see and do!

And just like the flower that you are, remember
to turn towards the sun,

Be brave and you will blossom - and with it,
have lots and lots of fun!

Dad & The Mountains

Come sun, rain, snow or mist; the mountains call
and Dad can't resist,
Putting on the gear and heading outside,
To feel nature's power with a step or a slide.

To know that his body, that he still commands,
Can achieve his ambitions without falling apart.
And that when tested, his resilience and courage
emerge,
Just like the sun's smile that looks down upon
the Earth.

It's the element of challenge that mountains
present,
Climbing upwards to the clouds or skiing down
the descent.
The peaks or the pistes; they both present a
journey.
And only those prepared, are ever really worthy,
Of becoming the person to achieve and to
conquer -
The reward is becoming, an epic explorer!

The mountains are a rollercoaster, full of highs
and lows,

Such as life itself with delights and knock-down
blows.
The struggle is real; some people give up,
but, just as in life, others can pick you up.

So Dad, never try to conquer the mountains
alone,
Climbing to a summit or skiing down below.
Take someone with you to share the mountain
terrain,
Slow down life - step out the fast lane.

Connection to self; connection to the Earth,
Connection to loved ones - the mountains, all
this, they serve.
Breathe in that air; still the busy mind,
And treasure these moments that in the
mountains, you will find.

Marvellous Unassuming Mum

Quietly determined, gently strong,
Deeply loving; complex as a song.

Multi-faceted, multi-talented, never quite
believing
In her own power and worth, to inspire and
create meaning.

Mum can be a mystery; not revealing all her
history,
Not until you've earned her trust, and she feels
heard.
Only those who really deserve, get to see all of
our mum.

She is a thinker; a deep feeler; a writer and a
teacher,
A crafter, a creative and book-loving researcher.

She has a spirit of adventure and a wild side too
- she just needs the encouragement of those
around her and soon,
She says: 'that's it, I can, I will and I do!'

Mum sees the beauty in the world around; she
takes huge pleasure in listening to the sounds…
Loving her garden beneath the blazing sun,
Nurturing its growth - just as she has, with her
daughter and son.

Today we call our mother, our friend - someone
whose support and love, we can always depend.

Thank you mum for being wonderful you,
And in those times when you feel a bit blue,
Remember you have raised two independent,
happy souls who know and appreciate, all that
you do.

The Mocha Moment

Just sit for a moment please and grab your
favourite mug.
You just need a moment, please, to give yourself
an internal hug.

A hug in a mug, that's a mocha to me,
Slightly sweet, slightly bitter, warm and
deliciously creamy.

It warms the hands, the mouth, the inside too,
A little ceremony of pause, reflect - right, what's
next to do?

Before We Speak

So much to say,
So many opinions to be had,
Some people's comments make others incredibly
sad.

We all have a voice,
And yes, it's there to be used,
But it's not for filling up silence or for leading to
abuse.

Does every little thought and feeling need to be
shared and handed over?
Not everyone has the capacity to process,
experience the resulting pain and then recover.

If only we could listen more and speak a little
less,
A world more empathetic, understanding and far
less, distressed.

Glimmers Not Triggers

In a world of trauma, turbulence and triggers,
Why not refocus our energies on noticing those
glimmers?

Glimmers are not always glamorous; but they
are spectacularly special,
They are the little big things that bring joy, and
unlock our true potential.

Glimmers are the tiny moments that evoke a
smile and bring clarity of thought,
They lower your heart rate, slow your breath and
bring the peace that you truly sought.

They are the holding of a hand or the sun's
caress on the skin,
Or the euphoric music moment that you get
completely lost within.

Glimmers can be external, bringing you back to
the present mo-ment,
Like noticing nature's artwork, and the flower's
alluring, delicious scent.

In our over stimulating world, with distractions
everywhere,
Sometimes we need a different lens, to see the
glimmers hiding, just there.

Our neuroception needs nurturing - it needs
rhythm and regulation,
Less flight, freeze or fight, more seeking
compromise and connection.

So prioritise finding these glimmers and adding
them to your life,
A life lived with glimmers has less darkness and
far more light.

Dear Future

Dear Future,

Thank you for inviting me Future,
I definitely want to come.

I can't wait to see you, be there and get busy.

I can't stop thinking about you, Future, I'm
constantly making plans for us. You are so
alluring, so seductive - you are the theme of my
dreams.

I know you are where my happiness is; where
I'll feel complete; where everything is, that I
could possibly want or need.

Oh Future, you promise me so much. If I just do
this and just do that, I know we'll be so happy
together.

I'll be there now, Future, I'm coming - I'm
already really there….

But, hang on, something's just arrived; there's a
knock at my door.

Oh! I have a gift, wow! It's PRESENT.

The Present - it's here, now, should I open it and look inside, or just come straight over, Future?

Let me read the label:

Dear You,

I hope this finds you well. I know you are eager to come and stay and be with me, but I'm not ready to host you just yet. I'm sad that you are missing out on the most beautiful, wonderful things that are right there, with you now. Have you met NOW? They are very special. Now has the most precious, expensive gift - it's the present moment for you to experience, sprinkled with some gratitude, which I'm informed, makes all the difference.

Enjoy.

Love from Future - I'll always be yours, here waiting.

xx

Dear Past

Dear Past,

Hello, how are you? Thank you for yesterday; I had a wonderful time.

Thank you for all the yesterdays - they have made me what I am today, and I feel truly grateful.

Past, how does it feel to be left behind? Does it get lonely back there? I don't mean to forge ahead without you, but I can't help it; it's just the way life is.

I do try and visit often - I love coming back to you to re-experience our many adventures. I find I do a lot of reflection, thinking and learning when I'm with you. I think that's a good thing.

I love looking at photos of our times together, that's why I take so many - so you are always with me, Past.

When I come and visit, I'm lucky enough to not really bump into Regret - I'm not keen on them.

Regret can cause problems and feelings of
unease - they cause an itch that can be difficult
to get rid of.

I try to avoid Regret as they are not something I
really want in my life - certainly not with this
gift I currently have: my time with Present.

Thank you, Past, for teaching me so much.

I feel wiser because of you.

I feel stronger because of you.

I feel powerful because of you.

You have been a tremendous teacher - you have
your subtle methods of helping me remember
the important things - they are ingrained on my
mind and hollowed into my heart.

But you let me forget the not-so-wonderful,
challenging times. Thank you for this.

Past, you have shown me where I have started,
and how far I have come - it's been a joyful
journey - it really has. But I'm far from the
finishing line; I'm not even half way. Hurray!

I have another good friend, who demands some of my time: they are called Future. I sometimes feel pulled in both directions, by you, Past, and by Future. It can be a struggle to remain, here, where I should be. Here, with Present.

I think, as I get older, I will be able to spend more time with you, Past. You will grow in size and superiority.

At the very end, Past, will you be with me? I hope so, Please? I know I'll need you so very much.

Bring all the photos of us, Past, just in case my memory lets me down.

Thank you for being just there, Past - you've got my back.

I just feel it and I know, you won't let me down.

Love from Me x

Paradoxes of Life

As I get older and hopefully wiser, I become
increasingly aware,

That there are many life paradoxes, apparent,
everywhere.

Observations of things, opposed to common
sense and yet, true.

They are really quite powerful and impactful -
really, they are - who knew?!

The Persuasion Paradox

The most persuasive people, do not overtly or
loudly persuade,
They listen, they observe, never argue or badly
behave.

They influence through example, connect
through the emotional,
Before you realise it, you are being led; their
influence, undeniable.

The Wisdom Paradox

Albert Einstein once said: "The more I learn, the
more I realise how much I don't know."
Isn't this true? Isn't it just so?

Don't be frightened by this; don't let it
overwhelm yourself,
We are not meant to know everything, merely
question, and delve.

Life long learning, is the route we should all
take,
Wisdom comes from awareness, reflection, and
even heartache.

The more I learn, and the more seeds I sow, the
stronger I feel: the wonder of the 'unknown'.

And finally,

The Death Paradox

Imagine your death, to truly live your life right,

Acknowledge the inescapability of death (at
least from this life).

By realising an end, will eventually come to us
all,
We can make life changes, no matter how big or
small.

And gain a perspective, a better world-view or
understanding,
That gives us more intention in our lives, and is
significantly life-enhancing.

We Write Our Own Stories

We write our own stories,
We turn each, individual page.

Chapter after chapter, we create every single
stage,
Of our own lives.

Choice by choice, each sentence is formed,
Punctuated by drama; with exclamation, comma
or delicate Letter drawn.

We pick up that pen and write the journey we are
about to take,
Selecting each perfect word or erasing another
mistake.

It is only at the end of our story can we look
back and decide on the title of our masterpiece.

Did we write a romance, a comedy or tragedy?

Perhaps we'll let others read it for themselves
and decide.

I know that I'm just glad to have made a mark; committed something to paper.

My book. My story. I have lived.

When The Show Is Over

At the end of my life, I already know,
What I'll be thinking and feeling - It's the end of
my show.

But the stage has been mine, for such a long
time,
I've enjoyed my moments in the spot light -I've
had my opportunity to shine.

I just want to have mattered, if only to a few,
To have warmed some hearts and be talked
about
 By those who I really knew…

I hope I take with me some of the energy I was
gifted at birth,
It's served me so well, and given me a strong
sense of my worth.

We are all energy and particles, after all,
Transferring it with every interaction,
No matter how big or small.

So, with this energy and power, I hope I've lit
light bulbs, Not extinguished any flames,

And after I've gone, and stepped off this stage,
I hope you will remember, more than just my
name.

www.ingramcontent.com/pod-product-compliance
Lightning Source LLC
Chambersburg PA
CBHW071235140726
47996CB00007B/2612